CHASING DREAMS

CHASING DREAMS

An Entrepreneur's Guide to Finance

TOM HAMPTON

ISBN: 978-1-954102-09-5
Library of Congress Control Number: 2023937326

Printed in the United States of America

First Printing: 2023
Edited by Kate Johnston, Eileen Maddocks, Beth Rule
Interior design by Amit Dey
Cover design by Veronica Coello

SOMETHING OR OTHER PUBLISHING LLC
Brooklyn, Wisconsin 53521
Info@SOOPLLC.com

For bulk orders e-mail: Orders@SOOPLLC.com

CONTENTS

INTRODUCTION

So, you want to be an entrepreneur! It's exciting to chase a dream. But at the end of the day, if you're going to be an entrepreneur, you need to know:

1. How much money is needed to start a business?
2. Am I making money?

We are going to help you understand what financial tools you need to use as an entrepreneur, such as a Profit & Loss Statement.

I know you're probably saying "But I have no idea what a Profit & Loss Statement is."

Don't worry! We will teach you that and other information too, and we will keep it simple.

You do not need to be a finance guru, but you do need to know some basics. Too often, financial professionals speak in a language the rest of the world has trouble understanding.

We are going to help you translate "financial speak" into a language you can easily grasp.

Let's get started!

1

HOW MUCH MONEY DO I NEED TO START A BUSINESS?

All aspiring entrepreneurs will need as much money as possible to get their businesses started, and you will need to show an investor, bank, or yourself how you are going to spend the money.

There are three buckets of money you need to understand and develop:

1. **Living Capital**—This is the money you, or you and your family, need to live adequately for one year.

2. **Working Capital**—Once you start the business, you will need money to operate it for at least a year. Never make your first year optimistic, but be prepared to deal with the growth if it comes quickly. You will need money for the weekly payroll, services, utilities, rent, insurance, advertising, shipping, and so forth.

   Why? Because you have to pay others before you get paid.

3. **Start-up Capital**—How much equipment do I need? What permits do I need? What will it cost me to get my facility ready? What expertise do I need before I start? How much inventory is required?

This first bucket of money is commonly overlooked or underfunded because the entrepreneur is usually afraid to explore what it would take to live comfortably. Somehow, entrepreneurs feel the need to suffer. Don't!!!! Starting a business can make you suffer enough. In fact, you will be much more productive in your business if you don't have to worry about basic living expenses.

Most businesses fail due to inadequate funding. The investor/bank is usually unforgiving unless you demonstrate in advance that you understand your funding needs. Don't be optimistic. Give yourself room for error.

That's why understanding these three buckets of money and being able to put them to work for you is critical to giving your business a better chance at success.

The first step we'll take is to explore two financial tools called a Profit & Loss Statement (P&L) and a Balance Sheet (B/S).

You can use your current financial life to learn these tools and practice them before you actually launch your business.

2

MY LIFE IS A PROFIT & LOSS STATEMENT

We will begin with our would-be entrepreneur Stephanie, who asked, "What is a Profit and Loss Statement (P&L)?" Below is a P&L.

Company Name Profit & Loss Statement January - December [Year]	
SALES	
Product & services	$0
Total Sales	**$0**
Less:	
EXPENSES	
Direct Product Expenses (DPE)*	**$0**
Gross Profit	**$0**
Operating Expenses	$0
Rent	0
Employee Labor	0
Insurance	0
Accounting	0
Marketing & Advertising	0
Legal, G&A, Other	0
Total Operating Expenses	**$0**
Net Operating Profit/(Loss)	**$0**
TAXES	**$0**
Profit/(Loss)	**$0**

*Direct Product Expenses are also known in Finance as
Cost of Goods Sold (COGS)

A P&L is made up of three parts as follows:

Profit & Loss Statement (P&L) Parts
Part 1 — Sales (What You Sold)
Part 2 — Expenses (Costs Incurred)
Part 3 — Taxes

It simply tells you whether you made money or not. You can use it to examine how much money you earned and how much money you spent.

PART 1 — SALES

Stephanie is married with two kids and her spouse is a stay-at-home dad. Stephanie makes $85,000 a year and pays $3,000 in state taxes and $12,000 in federal taxes.

Is that all the money that comes into the home?

No. Stephanie invested in three-year Certificates of Deposits (CDs),* from which she earns $8,000 a year. She pays $300 in state taxes and $900 in federal taxes on these investments a year.

Now Stephanie can determine her Family Sales as follows:

Stephanie's Family Sales	
Salary	$85,000
CDs	8,000
Total Family Sales	**$93,000**

The **gross amount** you earn is your sales line for a Family P&L. It is always more fun to start with "Sales" and growth opportunities.

---

* Note: Stock Dividends, Interest on Banking Accounts, and Interest on Bonds are other examples of additional personal income.

Nobody likes talking about expenses first.

In many other financial examples, when you see "Revenue," think SALES, SALES, SALES as an entrepreneur.

Make sure you continuously think about many ways to grow the business SALES. Identify as many streams of SALES as possible and you can attach the expenses/funding needed for each SALES stream.

PART 2 — EXPENSES

Now let's tackle the second part of the P&L statement: How much money did Stephanie's family spend on expenses monthly?

Stephanie and her spouse sat down and identified all the different bills they pay monthly.

Stephanie's Family Monthly Expenses	
Rent	$1,500
Car Note	400
Telephones	300
Healthcare	700
School	200
Gasoline	600
Utilities	400
Car Repair/Fuel	400
Insurance	100
Groceries	600
Cable TV	100
Entertainment	200
Clothing	200
Miscellaneous	300
Total Monthly Expenses	**$6,000**

Once they tallied up the total, they learned how much money they spent that month, $6,000.

This is the **EXPENSES** part of the P&L statement.

To get the **Total Year Expense**, we will multiply each category by twelve.

Stephanie's Family Yearly Expenses			
EXPENSES	**Monthly**	**Multipier**	**Yearly**
Rent	$1,500	12	$18,000
Car Note	400	12	4,800
Telephones	300	12	3,600
Healthcare	700	12	8,400
School	200	12	2,400
Gasoline	600	12	7,200
Utilities	400	12	4,800
Car Repair/Fuel	400	12	4,800
Insurance	100	12	1,200
Groceries	600	12	7,200
Cable TV	100	12	1,200
Entertainment	200	12	2,400
Clothing	200	12	2,400
Miscellaneous	300	12	3,600
Total	**$6,000**		**$72,000**

PART 3 — TAXES

But we still have one more expense to pay—the dreaded Tax Man.

To complete our tax payment, we refer to Stephanie's **PART 1 — SALES** where taxes were identified:

Stephanie's Family Taxes			
Segment	**Salary**	**CD**	**Total**
Federal	$12,000	$900	$12,900
State	3,000	300	3,300
Total Taxes	**$15,000**	**$1,200**	**$16,200**

Never treat what you potentially owe in taxes as a given. You can develop strategies to minimize your tax burden.

STEPHANIE'S FAMILY P&L

We can now build a P&L from the family's household financials:

Stephanie's Family P&L	
Sales (Income)	$93,000
Less:	
Expenses	-72,000
Taxes	-16,200
Profit/(Loss)*	$4,800

*A negative number indicates a loss.

Stephanie's family makes a profit and can save/invest $4,800 per year. In financial terms, profit and net income are one and the same.

We identified at the beginning of Chapter 1 the three buckets of money needed to start a business:

Buckets of Money Needed to Start a Business
1. LIVING CAPITAL
2. WORKING CAPITAL
3. START-UP CAPITAL

This information from her Family P&L statement helps Stephanie understand how much money she needs for **LIVING CAPITAL**. To live comfortably for a year, she needs $72,000 in cash, after taxes. If she wants to be conservative, she could add a 10% contingency to make it $79,200 for unknowns.

You can use the P&L tool for your household to practice being a CEO before you start a business.

Now let's look at Stephanie's completed P&L:

Company Name Profit & Loss Statement (P&L) January - December [Year]	
SALES (INCOME)	
Salary	$85,000
CDs	8,000
Total Sales	**$93,000**
Less:	
EXPENSES	
Rent	$18,000
Car Note	4,800
Telephones	3,600
Healthcare	8,400
School	2,400
Gasoline	7,200
Utilities	4,800
Car Repair/Fuel	4,800
Insurance	1,200
Groceries	7,200
Cable TV	1,200
Entertainment	2,400
Clothing	2,400
Miscellaneous	3,600
Total Operating Expenses	**$72,000**
Net Operating Profit/(Loss)	**$21,000**
TAXES	
State	$12,900
Federal	3,300
Total Taxes	**$16,200**
Profit/(Loss)	**$4,800**

3

MY LIFE IS A
BALANCE SHEET

Let's look at Stephanie's Balance Sheet (B/S). Below is a form for a typical B/S.

The B/S has two sides, **SIDE 1 (Total Assets)** and **SIDE 2 (Total Liabilities & Equity)**.

Company Name Balance as of [Date]			
Current Assets		**Short-term Debt**	
Cash	$0	Credit cards	$0
Inventory	0	Other payables	0
Accounts receivable	0	**Total Current Debt**	**$0**
Total Current Assets	**$0**		
		Long-term Debt	
Fixed Assets		Loans	0
Machinery & Equipment	0	**Total Long-term Debt**	**$0**
Buildings & Land	0	**Total Debt (Liabilities)**	**$0**
Total Fixed Assets	**$0**		
		Owner's Equity	**$0**
Total Assets	**$0**	**Total Liabilities & Owner's Equity**	**$0**
SIDE 1 = Total Assets		**SIDE 2 = Total Liabilities & Equity**	

Both sides of the B/S must always be equal.

SIDE 1 = SIDE 2

Total Assets = Total Liabilities + Equity

The B/S is a tool that summarizes what **Capital Items** you have. What are capital items? They include assets as follows:

- Cash you have on hand (Current Asset)
- Money customers owe you (Accounts Receivable - Current Asset)
- Materials you need to purchase (Inventory - Current Asset)
- Equipment you need to purchase to make the product (Machinery and Equipment - Property and Equipment)
- Computers, software, phones, and other IT equipment you need to purchase to operate the business (Machinery and Equipment)
- Vehicles you need to purchase (Machinery and Equipment)
- Facilities you need to purchase (Buildings and Land)
- Debt you owe others now (Accounts Payable - Current Liability)
- Debt you owe others over multiple years (Long-term Debt)
- Stocks you have sold (Owner's Equity)

First, we will identify what capital items are in **SIDE 1 — Total Assets**.

Total Assets fall into two categories:

TYPES OF ASSETS	TYPES OF CAPITAL ITEMS
CURRENT	Cash, CDs, Accounts Receivable (what customers owe), Materials, Supplies
FIXED	Equipment, Facilities, Cars, TVs, Computers, Software, Furniture

We need to separate the two categories because they serve two different purposes.

Current assets can be used to pay bills, buy materials, collect from customers, and so forth. **Current assets (cash or cash availability) will be KING as you start a business.**

Fixed assets are used long-term or over multiple years for things you utilize day in and day out to help make the product or perform the service such as the facility you work in, computers and software you use, or the forklift you drive.

Let's separate Stephanie's assets into two categories, **Current and Fixed Assets**.

First, we will work on **Current Assets**. Those Capital Items for her are the cash in her bank account and the $50,000 in CDs she invested.

Stephanie's Current Assets	
Capital Item	**Value**
Cash	$1,000
CDs	50,000
Total Current Assets	**$51,000**

The good news is that the liquid assets are easy to determine and will be the major area of focus for Stephanie, our CEO-entrepreneur, as she begins her journey.

Next are the **Fixed Assets**, which for simplicity's sake we are going to assign the following values:

Stephanie's Fixed Assets	
Capital Item	**Value**
2 Cars	$40,000
Furniture	10,000
Jewelry	3,000
Clothing	6,000
TVs/Computers	3,000
Total Fixed Assets	**$62,000**

The bad news is that the fixed asset side is not as easy to determine. However, do not spend too much time here. You will deal with this category when specific questions arise, such as: Do I need to buy a new car for the sales force? Should I purchase a facility?

You can use sites like eBay, Amazon, or Kelly's Blue Book to determine values for what these items are worth now.

The key here is to find out what you could sell the capital items for now. That number will give you the current market value.

Always remember that **cash or cash availability will be KING** as you start a business.

Fixed assets are not the primary focus initially. Many fixed assets can also be leased as an expense.

We can now build SIDE 1 of Stephanie's B/S.

Stephanie's Current Assets	
Capital Item	Value
Cash	$1,000
CDs	50,000
Total Current Assets	$51,000

Stephanie's Fixed Assets	
Capital Item	Value
2 Cars	$40,000
Furniture	10,000
Jewelry	3,000
Clothing	6,000
TVs/Computers	3,000
Total Fixed Assets	$62,000

Stephanie's Total Assets	
Total Assets	$113,000

We will take the work completed by Stephanie's Family and simply align the tables in vertical order and you have SIDE 1 of the B/S.

Stephanie's Current Assets	
Capital Item	Value
Cash	$1,000
CDs	50,000
Total Current Assets	$51,000
Stephanie's Fixed Assets	
Capital Item	Value
2 Cars	$40,000
Furniture	10,000
Jewelry	3,000
Clothing	6,000
TVs/Computers	3,000
Total Fixed Assets	$62,000
Stephanie's Total Assets	
Total Assets	$113,000

SIDE 1 = Total Assets	
Current Assets	Value
Cash	$1,000
CDs	50,000
Total Current Assets	$51,000
Fixed Assets	
Machinery & Equipment	$62,000
Total Fixed Assets	$62,000
Total Assets	$113,000

Remember that both sides of the Balance Sheet must be equal.

Now we will work on **SIDE 2 — Total Liabilities and Equity**, starting with liabilities.

The **Capital Item** for liabilities is **Debt**, what you owe.

Debt is both short-term and long-term.

TYPES OF DEBT	TYPES OF CAPITAL ITEMS
SHORT-TERM	Debt you have to pay off completely within a year (short-term loans, credit cards)
LONG-TERM	Debt that takes over one year to pay off (Equipment, Facilities, Cars, Computers, Software, Furniture)

Stephanie has $3,000 in credit card debt (short-term debt). She owes $20,000 on the cars and $4,000 on furniture (long-term debt).

Stephanie's Total Liabilities	
Capital Item	**Value**
Short-term Debt	
Credit Cards	3,000
Total Short-term Debt	**$3,000**
Long-term Debt	
Car Loan	20,000
Furniture	4,000
Total Long-term Debt	**$24,000**
Total Liabilities	**$27,000**

Credit card debt belongs in the short-term column; it should never be used to finance fixed assets (cars, equipment, and so forth).

Let's be frank and clear. If you have to use a credit card for fixed assets, usually that is a sign that you are in financial trouble (robbing Peter to pay Paul). There are usually better financing alternatives.

However, if you have the discipline to pay off your credit card monthly **IN FULL** for expenses that vary with sales, that will help you track those expenses easily and no credit card debt is built up.

Let's Recap:

- The B/S has two sides, SIDE 1 - Total Assets and SIDE 2 - Total Liabilities & Equity.

- Both sides of the B/S must always be equal.

SIDE 1 = SIDE 2

Total Assets = Total Liabilities + Equity

Stephanie knows that her Total Assets equal $113,000 and that her Total Liabilities equal $27,000. Now she can easily calculate Equity as follows:

Total Assets	-	Total Liabilities	=	Equity
$113,000	-	$27,000	=	$86,000

Now let's look at Stephanie's completed Balance Sheet:

Stephanie's Balance Sheet			
Current Assets		**Short-term Debt**	
Cash	$1,000	Credit cards	$3,000
CDs	50,000		
Total Current Assets	**$51,000**	**Total Current Debt**	**$3,000**
Fixed Assets		**Long-term Debt**	
Machinery & Equipment	62,000	Car loan	20,000
Toal Fixed Assets	**$62,000**	Furniture	4,000
		Total Long-term Debt	**$24,000**
		Total Debt (Liabilities)	**$27,000**
		Owner's Equity	**$86,000**
Total Assets	**$113,000**	**Total Liabilities & Owner's Equity**	**$113,000**
SIDE 1 = Total Assets		**SIDE 2 = Total Liabilities & Equity**	

Stephanie has a P&L and B/S. She can manage her household budget/assets and, after some practice, she will be ready to start a sporting business.

4

THE MONEY I NEED TO START A BUSINESS

As we stated in Chapter 1, there are three buckets of money you need to understand and develop:

Buckets of Money Needed to Start a Business
1. LIVING CAPITAL
2. WORKING CAPITAL
3. START-UP CAPITAL

Stephanie practiced for two years managing her own P&L and is now ready to start her sporting business **Big Sports**.

She knows she needs **$79,200 for Bucket #1: Living Capital.** Let's see what tools are needed for the other two buckets.

First, she needs the first year's P&L, which will let her know:

"How much money will she bring in and how much money will she spend?"

While we can make this very complicated, we will not. Let's review the parts of the P&L:

Profit & Loss Statement (P&L) Parts
Part 1 — Sales (What You Sold)
Part 2 — Expenses (Costs Incurred)
Part 3 — Taxes

PART 1— SALES

The first area to understand is always the market that you are selling into and its potential size. You cannot determine your financial needs or the viability of a business without this first step.

Stephanie has determined that a "niche or specialty strategy" will succeed, not a commodity sporting goods store.

Stephanie has done her research and has taken a night job in a sporting goods store to understand the market and expenses.

We are going to leverage her knowledge and take a very simple approach by quarter to determine the sales in Year 1.

First Quarter Sales

Based upon her experience in sporting goods stores, Stephanie estimates that when she opens the store, she will have about twenty-five customers a day, spending $50 a day. Her store will be open twenty days a month, so her first quarter sales are estimated to be:

25 (customers) * 3 (months) * 20 (days) * $50/customer = $75,000

Second Quarter Sales

Stephanie estimates in the second quarter she will have about fifty customers a day, spending $50/day.

50 (customers) * 3 (months) * 20 (days) * $50/customer = $150,000

Third Quarter Sales

Stephanie estimates in the third quarter she will have about seventy-five customers a day, spending $50 a day.

75 (customers) * 3 (months) * 20 (days) * $50/customer = $225,000

Fourth Quarter Sales

Stephanie estimates in the fourth quarter she will have about 100 customers a day, spending $50 a day.

100 (customers) * 3 (months) * 20 (days) * $50/customer = $300,000

While we have sales estimates, they are notoriously inaccurate. Always be conservative with your sales expectations in the first year. If they match or exceed your forecast, that's great! You can always get more cash when you have more sales.

Big Sports Year 1 Sales	
Quarterly Sales	**Amount**
Q1	$75,000
Q2	150,000
Q3	225,000
Q4	300,000
Total Year 1 Sales	**$750,000**

Again, make sure that you continually think about various new ways to grow the business, thus increasing your Sales. Identify the sales streams and attach the expenses and funding needed for each sales stream. Understanding the top line always comes first.

Now that we have our sales forecast, we can figure out **Part 2 — Expenses**.

PART 2 — EXPENSES

Remember, we need to align sales streams with the appropriate expenses. In Stephanie's case, she has one stream: sports.

Stephanie needs a facility, people to run the store, and many other basics just like her household expenses, as follows:

Big Sports Expenses
Direct Product Expense (DPE)
Rent
Employee Labor
Insurance
Utilities
Accounting
Legal
Cell Phone, Software, IT
Office Supplies
Healthcare
Credit Card Expense
Marketing/Advertising

We will begin with Rent and save the Direct Product Expense (DPE) for last.

Rent

Stephanie decides she needs a 10,000-square-foot facility in a place with high foot traffic. She found a location where she could rent the space monthly for $1/sq. ft. or $10K/month.

Employee Labor

Stephanie's store will be open from 10 a.m. to 9 p.m. She plans on having two other employees cover the store.

To guarantee to find good help, she will pay $15/hour.

She will have one employee work eight-hour shifts from 8 a.m. to 4 p.m. and the other from 2 p.m. to 10 p.m., which will result in a daily expense of:

$$\$15/hour * 8(hours) * 2(employees) = \$240/day$$

Stephanie will keep her store open twenty days a month, which makes her monthly store labor expense:

$$20 \text{ days} * \$240/day = \$4,800$$
$$(\text{Let's round up to } \$5,000/month.)$$

Always pay a little more to get good employees because they will make your life and work so much easier.

Insurance

Two types of insurance are usually recommended:

1. Business Owner Insurance (bundles business interruption, property, vehicle, liability, and crime)
2. Workers Compensation Insurance (only if you have employees)

The best quotes were for $300 a month for Business Owner Insurance and $50 a month per employee for Workers' Compensation Insurance.

Note your insurance cost will vary by type of business, age of owner, city/state, how much employees are paid, and many more factors. Shop for the best deal, but use a quality company.

Utilities, Accounting, Legal, Office Supplies, Cell Phone/Software/IT

Stephanie also estimated that her monthly utilities will be $100 a month, accounting (outsourced) will be $300 a month, legal will be $200 a month, Cell Phone/Software/IT in the store will be $1000 a month, and office supplies will be $100 a month.

Segment	Amount
Utilities	$100
Accounting	300
Legal	200
Office Supplies	100
Cell Phone, Software, IT	$1,000

Healthcare

Healthcare plans vary considerably by insurance company and what level of health insurance you select. Stephanie has elected a standard health plan, with co-pays, for $1,500 a month.

Credit Card Expense

Since Stephanie has retail customers, she needs the ability to process credit cards. She found out the expense varies significantly among suppliers. She chose one whose price is based upon a percentage of the sale, and since her business is a start-up, she will pay 2% per sale.

Marketing & Advertising

Her marketing and advertising costs include social media and an online selling presence. She outsourced these (makes it easy) to a Marketing/Outbound Telemarketing firm which will charge her $1,000 per month. It is very important to gain visibility with customers for a start-up.

Make sure you focus on how you are going to get customers to buy your product. Forget finance if you can't attract customers to obtain sales. Finance is an outcome of your business, not the driver.

Direct Product Expense

The final piece of the puzzle is the cost to make the product, which we will call the Direct Product Expense (DPE); Stephanie will need the forecasted sales and the gross margin.

If you do not know what the gross margin is on your products, take the time to learn. This can easily "make or break" your business profitability. The gross margin is also referred to in finance as the gross profit. It is defined as:

Gross Margin = Sales – Direct Product Expense (DPE)

DPE is the direct labor and materials required to make the product.

Stephanie now has all the expenses except for the DPE associated with sales. To calculate this, she will use the previously forecasted sales by quarter.

Remember, many individuals will try to predict month-to-month sales, which will always be wrong. We are trying a new approach and only predicting the sales by quarter.

To calculate the DPE, we will use our Gross Margin.

Gross Margin = Sales – Direct Product Expense (DPE)

In Stephanie's case, her work in the sporting goods store showed her that she could achieve a 45% Gross Margin on 90% of the products. (Don't overanalyze – use 0.45 or 45%.)

The DPE can now be calculated with sales being 1 or 100%.

$$\text{Gross Margin} = \text{Sales} - \text{Direct Product Expenses (DPE)}$$
$$0.45 \quad = \quad 1 \quad - \text{Direct Product Expenses (DPE)}$$
$$\downarrow \qquad\qquad \downarrow \qquad\qquad\qquad \downarrow$$
$$45\% \quad = 100\% - \text{Direct Product Expenses (DPE)}$$

The DPE equals 0.55 or 55%. The DPE = Sales * 0.55.

Note for every $1 of product that Stephanie sells, its DPE is 55 cents.

Multiply the sales by the DPE, i.e. for Q1 (75,000 * 0.55 = 41,250).

Big Sports Direct Product Expense (DPE)			
Quarter	Sales	% Cost	$ Cost
1	$75,000	55%	$41,250
2	150,000	55%	82,500
3	225,000	55%	123,750
4	300,000	55%	165,000
Total	$750,000	55%	$412,500

The approach we used is the easiest way to determine the DPE because it relies on your knowledge of the product cost and sales. However, if you know the per-unit material and labor cost of each product, simply add them together and multiply by the number of units. Given the number of products, this can be time-consuming

PART 3 — TAXES

The last area is **Part 3 — Taxes**, your tax rate will vary based on your financial situation. Stephanie assumes a 35% tax rate, which includes both Federal and State Taxes.

She now has everything she needs to forecast her P&L in year 1.

Again, we will not try to predict the month-to-month P&L. Let's continue our new approach and only predict the P&L by quarter.

Now we have Parts 1 and 2 of the P&L:

1. The Quarterly Sales

Big Sports Year 1 Sales	
Quarterly Sales	**Amount**
Q1	$75,000
Q2	150,000
Q3	225,000
Q4	300,000
Total Year 1 Sales	**$750,000**

2. Big Sports Expenses by Month, which we will convert to quarterly.

Big Sports Monthly Expenses	
	Amount
Direct Product Expense (DPE)	% of Sales
Monthly Expenses:	
Rent	$10,000
Employee Labor	5,000
Insurance	400
Utilities	100
Accounting	300
Legal	200
Cell Phone, Software, IT	1,000
Office Supplies	100
Healthcare	1,500
Credit Card Expense	% of Sales
Marketing/Advertising	1,000
Total per Month	**$19,600**

Note expenses like labor, insurance, rent, legal, and office supplies are what we will call primarily static because they do not change from month to month. In finance, these are called operating or fixed expenses.

We can determine Big Sports expenses for each quarter by simply multiplying each monthly expense by 3, except for Credit Card and DPE, which vary with sales.

Big Sports Quarterly Expenses			
Quarterly Sales			**$75,000**
Direct Product Expense (DPE)	% of Sales	55%	$41,250
Operating Expenses	**Monthly**	**Multiplier**	**Quarterly**
Rent	$10,000	3	$30,000
Employee Labor	5,000	3	15,000
Insurance	400	3	1,200
Utilities	100	3	300
Accounting	300	3	900
Legal	200	3	600
Cell Phone, Software, IT	1,000	3	3,000
Office Supplies	100	3	300
Healthcare	1,500	3	4,500
Credit Card Expense	% of Sales	2%	1,500
Marketing/Advertising	1,000	3	3,000
Total per Month	**$19,600**		**$60,300**

BIG SPORTS P&L — YEAR 1

We can now build Big Sports P&L in Year 1.

BIG SPORTS YEAR 1 P&L					
	Q1	Q2	Q3	Q4	Total
SALES	$75,000	$150,000	$225,000	$300,000	$750,000
EXPENSES					
Direct Product Expense	41,250	82,500	123,750	165,000	412,500
Gross Profit ($)	**$33,750**	**$67,500**	**$101,250**	**$135,000**	**$337,500**
Gross Profit (%)	**45.0%**	**45.0%**	**45.0%**	**45.0%**	**45.0%**
Operating Expenses					
Rent	30,000	30,000	30,000	$30,000	$120,000
Employee Labor	15,000	15,000	15,000	$15,000	$60,000
Insurance	1,200	1,200	1,200	$1,200	$4,800
Utilities	300	300	300	$300	$1,200
Accounting	900	900	900	900	3,600
Legal	600	600	600	600	600
Cell Phone, Software, IT	3,000	3,000	3,000	3,000	3,000
Office Supplies	300	300	300	300	300
Healthcare	4,500	4,500	4,500	4,500	4,500
Credit Card Expense	1,500	3,000	4,500	6,000	15,000
Marketing/Advertising	3,000	3,000	3,000	3,000	3,000
Total Operating Expenses	**$60,300**	**$61,800**	**$63,300**	**$64,800**	**$250,200**
Net Operating Profit/(Loss)	**($26,550)**	**$5,700**	**$37,950**	**$70,200**	**$87,300**
TAXES @ 35%	($9,293)	$1,995	$13,283	$24,570	$21,825
Profit/(Loss)	**($17,258)**	**$3,705**	**$24,668**	**$45,630**	**$65,475**

Note: Numbers presented in parenthesis ( ) are negative.

SECOND BUCKET — WORKING CAPITAL

Stephanie now has a Big Sports P&L. She will use her P&L to help determine the **Second Bucket — Working Capital**, which is the money to pay store labor and operating expenses to operate the store for at least a year.

The key is to use the Big Sports P&L she has developed. The formula we will use is as follows:

(Qtr Labor + Qtr Operating Expenses) * 2 = Working Capital

Big Sports Working Capital			
Quarterly Sales			**$75,000**
Direct Product Expense (DPE)	% of Sales	55%	$41,250
Operating Expenses	**Quarterly**	**Multiplier**	**TOTAL**
Rent	$30,000	2	$60,000
Employee Labor	15,000	2	30,000
Insurance	1,200	2	2,400
Utilities	300	2	600
Accounting	900	2	1,800
Legal	600	2	1,200
Cell Phone, Software, IT	3,000	2	6,000
Office Supplies	300	2	600
Healthcare	4,500	2	9,000
Credit Card Expense	1,500	2%	N/A
Marketing/Advertising	3,000	2	6,000
Total per Month	**$60,300**		**$117,600**

While Stephanie is happy with the money she will make in year 1, her money needs are not over.

The **Third Bucket** is **Start-up Capital**.

To determine this, we need the B/S with assets being the primary focus (capital items/inventory).

THIRD BUCKET — START-UP CAPITAL

Stephanie has done her homework on the Big Sports P&L. Now she will forecast her initial Balance Sheet.

To complete a Balance Sheet, she is going to determine her capital item costs. She needs the following:

Big Sports Start-Up Capital	
Laptop Computer	$1,500
Point of Sales system, with a Smart Cash Register, Barcode Scanner & Supplies	2,500
Office Furniture: Desk/ Chairs/ Filing Cabinets	500
8 12 ft. Gondola Shelving for the product	3,200
Ladders	100
In-House Inter-co/Phone System	200
Subtotal	**$8,000**

Stephanie now has the capital item costs to start her business, except for the inventory to keep the store stocked in the first year.

She can calculate the inventory by using the work completed in Big Sports P&L.

To accomplish this, we need to go back to the Big Sports P&L and get the Direct Product Expense (DPE).

BIG SPORTS START-UP CAPITAL INVENTORY					
	Q1	Q2	Q3	Q4	Total
Direct Product Expense	41,250	82,500	123,750	165,000	**$412,500**

To start your business, make sure that you have enough inventory to last the first year. To make it simple, forecast your initial inventory dollars required to equal one year of the DPE. In this case, it would equal $412,500.

As a result, her total Start-up Capital equals the $8,000 in equipment plus the $412,500 required for inventory in the first year.

Big Sports Start-Up Capital	
Laptop Computer	$1,500
Point of Sales system, with a Smart Cash Register, Barcode Scanner & Supplies	2,500
Office Furniture: Desk/ Chairs/ Filing Cabinets	500
8 12 ft. Gondola Shelving for the product	3,200
Ladders	100
In-House Inter-co/Phone System	200
Subtotal	**$8,000**
Inventory to stock the store	412,500
TOTAL START-UP CAPITAL	**$420,500**

While the inventory number looks high, not having a product on hand will kill a start-up quickly. If the business fails, cash can be generated by discounting the inventory to give funds back to the investors or banks. In many cases, banks and investors will provide multiple funding windows if they are aware of your total needs.

Now Stephanie can answer the question.

"How much money do I need to start my business?"

Stephanie needs $617,300 to give her business the best possible chance to succeed.

Big Sports Buckets of Money Needed to Start a Business	
1. LIVING CAPITAL	$79,200
2. WORKING CAPITAL	117,600
3. START-UP CAPITAL	420,500
TOTAL	**$617,300**

Again, most businesses fail due to inadequate funding. The investor/bank is usually unforgiving unless you demonstrate in advance that you understand your funding needs. Don't be optimistic. Give yourself room for error.

Investors and banks probably will not provide a loan for your total requirements upfront, but they will set in place funding mechanisms to address your total funding requirements. Remember, cash or cash availability will be KING.

It's easy to now build the starting Year 0 (start of the business) Balance Sheet to complete the cycle.

Big Sports Initial Balance Sheet (B/S)	
ASSETS	**Amount**
Cash	196,800
Inventory	412,500
Accounts Receivable	0
Current Assets	**$609,300**
Fixed Assets	**$8,000**
Total Assets	**$617,300**
LIABILITIES & EQUITY	
Accounts Payable	0
Short-Term Debt	0
Current Liabilities	0
Equity	**$617,300**
Total Liabilities & Equity	**$617,300**

5

DEVELOPING
A BUSINESS PLAN

A major benefit of the process described in this book is that it creates a business plan for you.

Let's define the components of a business plan.

1. The Executive Summary

The Executive Summary provides an overview of the business including details about what it offers. It's critical that the executive summary is outstanding, especially when seeking funding because it's a summary of the entire business plan.

2. The Business Description

A Business Description provides information about the business the entrepreneur is starting, including what sort of problems the product or services solve, who the most likely customer is, the team's expertise, and the business's competitive advantage.

3. Market Analysis

A market analysis helps the entrepreneur identify the best customers. In the market analysis, research the primary target market for the product or service, including geographic location, demographics, and the target market's needs with how these needs are currently being met.

4. Competitive Analysis

A competitive analysis defines how successful the direct and indirect competitors are in the marketplace plus an analysis of how the entrepreneur will overcome any entry barriers to the chosen market. The competitive analysis also needs to distinguish the business from the competition, which is especially important in persuading potential funding sources that the business will be able to compete in the marketplace.

5. **Sales and Marketing Plan**

   The sales and marketing section offers a detailed explanation of the entrepreneur's sales strategy, pricing plan, proposed advertising and promotional activities, and the benefits of the products or services offered. This is where the entrepreneur outlines the business's unique selling proposition, describes how it is going to get its goods and/or services to market, and explains why people would buy from this business rather than from the competition.

6. **Ownership and Management Plan**

   The outline of the business's legal structure and management resources will include the internal management team, external management resources, and human resources needs. It should also include the experience or special skills each person in the management team brings to the business.

7. **Operating Plan**

   The operating plan gives information on how the entrepreneur's business will be run. It provides a description of the business's physical location, facilities and equipment, kinds of employees needed, inventory requirements, suppliers, and any other applicable operating details, such as a description of the manufacturing process.

8. **Financial Plan**

   The entrepreneur's funding requirements:
   1. **Living Capital**
   2. **Working Capital**
   3. **Start-Up Capital**

   Additionally, a summary of cash needed to fund the business, a Profit & Loss Statement, and an initial Balance Sheet are usually required. Instructions for developing all of these are outlined in the book.

6

TRICKS OF THE TRADE & COMMONSENSE ADVICE

1. The Operating Cash Flow Ratio (OCFR) is another useful tool and it can be calculated by using the information from your B/S, defined as follows:

$$\frac{\text{CASH}}{\text{ACCOUNTS RECEIVABLE}}$$

You want the OCFR to be as close to, or greater than, 1. If it is lower than 0.5, you have twice as many receivables to collect as cash, which is a sign of cashflow troubles.

2. Always pay a little more to get good employees; they will make your life and work easier.

3. Make sure you focus on how you are going to get customers to buy your product. Forget finance, if you can't attract customers to obtain sales. Finance is an outcome of your business, not the driver.

4. Look at your expenses. How can you reduce your expenses and maintain quality to make more money? How much more money do you need or want to make? What is the plan to achieve that goal?

5. Note that your insurance cost will vary by type of business, age of owner, city/state, the income of the employees, and many more factors. Shop for the best deal but use a quality company.

6. Credit card debt should never be used to finance fixed assets such as cars and equipment. Let's be frank and clear. If you must use a credit card for fixed assets, that's usually a sign of financial trouble (robbing Peter to pay Paul). There are often better financing alternatives than high-interest credit cards.

7. If you have the discipline to pay off your credit card monthly for expenses that vary with sales, it will help you track those expenses easily without incurring credit card debt with high-interest liability.

8. If you do not know what the gross margin is on your products, take the time to learn. This can easily make or break your business.

9. Sales estimates are notoriously inaccurate. Always be conservative with your sales expectations in the first year. If they match or exceed your forecast, that's great. You can always get more cash when you have greater sales than forecast.

10. It's a must that you do your research on your type of business. Nothing beats hard work.

Commonsense Advice

- Use your job and your household budget to start managing a Profit and Loss Statement (P&L) and Balance Sheet (B/S).

- Don't wait until you want to start a business to manage budgets and P&Ls. Get started now!

- Take your time to hire good people; turnover will kill you quicker than overtime.

- Don't focus on the squeaky wheel (the complainer). Focus on the 90% of people who help you run your business.

- Family members' roles and salaries need to be clearly defined and priced against the market using online recruiting sites. Bringing in family members can be like adding a cancer to your life if not done wisely.

- "Pigs get fat; hogs get slaughtered." Don't get too greedy because it usually does not end well.

- Some say the definition of luck is when preparation meets opportunity; stay prepared.

- At the end of your business day, forget that day's problems. Instead, remember that day's blessings. Look for small wins every day.

- Most businesses fail due to inadequate funding. The investor/bank is usually unforgiving unless you demonstrate in advance that you understand your funding needs. Don't be optimistic; give yourself room for error.

- In every business, always remember this saying: "You never know what will be washed up on your shore today"—so, stay flexible and prepared.

This book is for your reference to help you quickly build the necessary financial tools to get started in business. It is hoped that it will also improve your decision-making process.

Don't give your book away. This book is a "how to" that you can always come back to over time.

Finally, while you may not be a financial guru now, you do know enough to ask your financial people the right business questions.

Go start making your $MILLIONS!!!

THANK YOU FOR PURCHASING

AND

GOOD LUCK!!!

ABOUT THE AUTHOR

My life's journey has taken me through many paths from an entrepreneur to a corporate executive and from small cities to major metropolises. I grew up with the opportunity to learn from my mother while observing my father and grandfather's entrepreneurial experience. It was this journey that has given me the insights, education, and experience to address the largest issue I have seen...a lack of financial literacy.

I started my journey in Houston, and at the age of 12, we moved to the "country" on the gulf coast of Mississippi with wild animals. I left the South and followed in my mother's footsteps, the first female to receive a master's degree in chemistry from Texas Southern University, by obtaining a Bachelor of Science in Electrical Engineering from Notre Dame. After graduating, I worked for Xerox in new product development as an engineer.

I then moved to the business side by going to Cornell University and obtaining an MBA in Finance and then taking a job in strategic planning with Scott Paper Company. My next move was to become an entrepreneur, which took me to Los Angeles to start small distribution companies with my business partner.

After a few years, the business didn't grow enough to support my partner and me, so I then went to work for Avery International, where my corporate career took off. My ability to take what is viewed as a complex topic, then explain it in simple forms that everyone can understand, was a major factor in my success. At Avery, I ran both financial and operating business units. My business unit competed against small businesses, where we went from $12 million to $20+ million in sales.

My desire to stay in California resulted in my moving to Southern California Edison managing the Real Estate Business Unit and introducing process/performance management to improve several organizations. After I retired from corporate America, I re-ignited my entrepreneurial spirit, and my wife and I started Stephanie & Tom Hampton Consulting where I focus on bringing the skills I have learned through my journey to small business CEOs. It became clear to me both in corporate America and entrepreneurial America that the big gap was not strategy or operations—it was financial literacy. *Chasing Dreams: An Entrepreneur's Guide to Finance* is my contribution to improving the business financial literacy of entrepreneurial America.